Hours in
the Garden
and Other Poems

BOOKS BY HERMANN HESSE

Hours in the Garden

and Other Poems

Hermann Hesse

Translated by
Rika Lesser

FARRAR · STRAUS · GIROUX
New York

Translated from the German. "Tagebuchblatt," "Pavillon im Winter," and "Skizzenblatt," copyright 1953 by Suhrkamp Verlag, Berlin; "Stunden im Garten" and "Der lahme Knabe," copyright 1952 by Suhrkamp Verlag, Frankfurt am Main; the text of the above included in *Gesammelte Schriften*, Fünfter Band, published by Suhrkamp Verlag, Berlin und Frankfurt/M, 1968. "Knarren eines geknickten Astes," from *Hermann Hesse zum Gedächtnis*, copyright © 1962 by Suhrkamp Verlag, Frankfurt am Main

Published simultaneously in Canada by
McGraw-Hill Ryerson Ltd., Toronto

Printed in the United States of America

Library of Congress Cataloging in Publication Data
Hesse, Hermann, 1877-1962.
Hours in the garden and other poems.
1. Gardens—Poetry. I. Lesser, Rika. II. Title.
PT2617.E85A24   1979   831'.9'12   78-27756

Contents

❧

Hours in
the Garden
and Other Poems

Tagebuchblatt

Am Abhang hinterm Hause hab ich heute
Durch Wurzelwerk und Steinicht eine Grube
Gehauen und gegraben, tief genug,
Und jeden Stein aus ihr entfernt und auch
Die spröde, dünne Erde weggetragen.
Dann kniet ich eine Stunde da und dort
Im alten Wald und sammelte mit Kelle
Und Händen aus vermoderten
Kastanienstrünken jene schwarze, mulmige
Walderde mit dem warmen Pilzgeruch,
Zwei schwere Kübel voll, trug sie hinüber
Und pflanzte in die Grube einen Baum,
Umgab ihn freundlich mit der torfigen Erde,
Goß sonngewärmtes Wasser langsam zu
Und schwemmte, schlämmte sanft die Wurzel ein.
Da steht er, klein und jung, und wird da stehen,
Wenn wir verschollen sind und unserer Tage
Lärmige Größe und unendliche Not
Vergessen ist und ihre irre Angst.

Föhn wird ihn beugen, Regenwind ihn zausen,
Sonne ihm lachen, nasser Schnee ihn drücken,
Zeisig und Kleiber werden ihn bewohnen,

Page from a Journal

❧

On the slope behind the house today
I cut through roots and rocks and
Dug a hole, deep and wide,
Carted away from it each stone
And all the friable, thin earth.
Then I knelt there a moment, walked
In the old woods, bent down again, using
A trowel and both my hands to scoop
Black, decaying woods-soil with the warm
Smell of fungi from the trunk of a rotting
Chestnut tree—two heavy buckets full I carried
Back to the hole and planted the tree inside;
Carefully I covered the roots with peaty soil,
Slowly poured sun-warmed water over them,
Mudding them gently until the soil settled.
It stands there, young and small,
Will go on standing when we are gone
And the huge uproar, endless urgency and
Fearful delirium of our days forgotten.

The föhn will bend it, rainstorms tear at it,
The sun will laugh, wet snow weigh it down,
The siskin and the nuthatch make it their home,

An seinem Fuß der stille Igel wühlen.
Und was er je erlebt, geschmeckt, erlitten,
Der Jahre Lauf, wechselnde Tiergeschlechter,
Bedrückung, Heilung, Wind- und Sonnenfreundschaft,
Wird täglich aus ihm strömen im Gesang
Des rauschenden Laubes, in der freundlichen
Gebärde seines sanften Wipfelwiegens,
Im zarten süßen Duft des harzigen Saftes,
Der seine schlafverklebten Knospen feuchtet,
Im ewigen Spiel der Lichter und der Schatten,
Das er zufrieden mit sich selber spielt.

1939

And the silent hedgehog burrow at its foot.
All it has ever experienced, tasted, suffered:
The course of years, generations of animals,
Oppression, recovery, friendship of sun and wind
Will pour forth each day in the song
Of its rustling foliage, in the friendly
Gesture of its gently swaying crown,
In the delicate sweet scent of resinous
Sap moistening the sleep-glued buds,
And in the eternal game of lights and
Shadows it plays with itself, content.

1939

Stunden im Garten

Eine Idylle

Morgens so gegen die sieben verlaß ich die Stube und trete
Erst auf die lichte Terrasse, dort brennt die Sonne
　　schon wacker
Zwischen den Schatten vom Feigenbaum, die rauhe granitne
Brüstung fühlt sich schon warm an. Hier liegt und wartet
　　mein Werkzeug,
Jedes Stück mir vertraut und befreundet: der runde Korb für
　　das Unkraut,
Die Zappetta, das Häckchen mit kurzem Stiel (zwischen Holze
　　und Eisen
Hab ich ein Streifchen Schuhleder gefügt, dem Rat eines alten
Klugen Tessiners folgend, auch halt ich im Feuchten
　　verwahrt es,
Daß es nicht klaffe und stets bereit sei, man braucht es
　　ja immer).
Auch ein Rechen steht hier und zu Zeiten Hacke und Spaten,
Gießkannen zwei, gefüllt mit sonnegewärmtem Wasser.
Korb und Häckchen nehm ich zur Hand und trete,
　　der Sonne entgegen,
Meinen Morgenweg an, an den schon verblühten und matten
Rosen vorüber und meinem Blumenwald bei der Treppe,
Wo um die Kletterrose, die am Granit sich emporrankt,
Vielerlei Blumen und Kräuter sich ineinander verwirren,

Hours in the Garden
An Idyll

❦

Toward seven o'clock every morning, I leave my study
    and step
Out on the bright terrace; the sun already burns resplendent
Between the shadows of the fig tree, makes the low wall
    of coarse
Granite warm to the touch. Here my tools lie ready
    and waiting,
Each one an intimate, an ally: the round basket for weeds;
The *zappetta*, the small hoe with a short haft (taking
    the advice
Of a clever old man of Ticino, I've put a strip of
Shoe leather between the wood and the iron; and I keep
    the tool
In a damp place so the wood won't split; you need it
    all the time).
There's a rake here as well, and at times a mattock
    and spade,
Or two watering cans filled with water warmed by the sun.
With my basket and small hoe in hand, facing the sun, I
Go out for my morning walk, passing the withered and spent
Roses, up to my forest of blooms by the staircase;
All kinds of flowers wind round the tendrils of the rambling
Roses that climb up the granite, tangling themselves in
    each other:

Gladiolen viele, und Frauenherz, echter Jasmin auch,
Natalinas Gabe, Arabis und Sonnenblumen, die sind hier
Zwar vom Winde gefährdet, ich muß bei jedem Gewitter,
Jedem Föhntag zittern um sie, und pflanzte sie dennoch,
Weil sie mir lieb sind und ich ihnen hier am öftsten begegne.
Bis ins vergangene Jahr stand hier auch, Fremdling im Grünen,
Ein gewaltiger Kaktus der Treppe nah, von der Größe
Eines zehnjährigen Knaben vielleicht; durch mehrere Jahre
Hielt er sich gut und wuchs stark und hielt mit
      bewaffneten Händen
Jegliche Nachbarschaft sich vom Leibe, nur unten am Fuße
Siedelte sich, wer weiß woher, ein bräunlicher,
      zwerghafter Klee an,
Den er duldete und mit ihm Kameradschaft zu haben
Sichtlich zufrieden war. Doch vorm Jahr im
      schneereichen Winter
Knickte die Schneelast ihm mehrere fleischige Zweige,
      und langsam
Drang von den Wunden her die Fäulnis fressend ins Innre.
Heut füllen kleinere Kräuter die traurige Lücke, und dort wo
Jener Fremdling einst wurzelte, pflanzt ich versuchsweis
Eine Akelei ein und hoffe, daß ihr der Ort nicht
Allzu sonnenreich sei, da ja ihre Heimat der Wald ist.
Nickend geh ich vorbei, doch schon nach wenigen Schritten
Auf dem Kiesplatz vorm Haus noch muß ich mich bücken,
      es grünen
Zwei, drei junge Kräutchen im Kies und es liegen,
      schon gilbend,
Frühgefallene Blätter von Feige und Maulbeer, die ich entferne,
Denn so will's das Gefühl: man halte so sauber den Garten,

Not a few gladioli, and bleeding heart, and jasmine,
Natalina's gift, Arabis and sunflowers—the wind
Threatens them all; each stormy day, every day the föhn
Blows, they worry me, and yet I planted them because
They are dear to me, and I find them here most of the time.
Until sometime last year, a stranger to these rural parts,
A mighty cactus stood near the staircase, about as tall
As a ten-year-old boy; for several years it held out
And grew strong, with armored hands it kept all society
At a distance; but below, at its foot, a brownish,
Dwarf-like clover settled in, almost unnoticed, which it
Tolerated, and with whose companionship the cactus
Was visibly content. But last winter the heavy load
Of snow burdened many of its fleshy branches, broke them.
Putrefaction pressed slowly from the wounds, eating its way
Inside. Today smaller plants fill the mournful hole, and
Where that armored stranger once struck root, tentatively I
Planted a columbine, and I hope there won't be too much
Sun for it here, because its home is the forest floor.
Nodding, I walk by, but after a few steps I must stoop down
Again; in front of the house, in the broad gravel bed
       two or three
Young weeds sprout up; around them, already yellowing,
      lie early
Fallen leaves of the fig and mulberry, which I clear away;
For feeling will have its way: the garden must be kept as tidy

Wie es nur eben gehn will, doch doppelt sauber ums Haus her,
Wo im Kiesplatz, im Rosenbeet und im Buchsbaum
    das Haus sich
Fortsetzt, und erst vom Buchs an der Garten richtig beginnet.

Durch die Reben den Grashang hinab, den Strohhut tief in
    der Stirne,
Steig ich die schöngelegten Steinstufen, Abhang um Abhang.
Schon ist verschwunden das Haus, ich seh den
    beschnittenen Buchsbaum
Starr in den glühenden Himmel ragen, es nimmt mich
    der Garten,
Nimmt mich der steile Rebenhang auf, und schon sind
    die Gedanken
Weg vom Hause, vom Frühstück, den Büchern, der Post und
    der Zeitung.
Einen Augenblick noch verlocket das Fernblau die Augen
Freundlich zum Blick ins Gebirg und über den gleißenden
    See hin,
Wo am Morgen die Berge so zart gestuft gegen's Licht stehn,
Welche dann, wie die Sonne dem Scheitel des Himmels
    sich nähert,
Fester, massiger, wirklicher werden und gegen den Abend
Warm bestrahlt sich erschließen und bunt in
    täuschender Nähe
Ihre Felsen und Wälder und Dörfer herzeigen im Goldlicht.
Jetzt am Morgen sind nur die großen Linien der Grate
Sichtbar und Gipfel, blaugrau die vordern, die hintern
    aufhellend

As possible, especially round the outside of the house,
For in the gravel bed, the rose beds, the boxtree,
  the house lives
On; only beyond the boxtree does the garden proper begin.

My straw hat low on my brow, I go down the grassy,
  vine-covered
Slope, mount the beautiful sloping stone stairs, step after step.
Already the house has vanished; I see the clipped boxwood
Tower rigid in the glowing sky, and the garden takes me,
The steep vineyard slope receives me; at once my thoughts are
Far from the house, from breakfast, books, mail and the paper.
For a moment more the distant blue amiably lures
My eyes across the glistening lake over into
The mountains, which, against the morning light, stand
  softly steplike;
When the sun nears zenith they become more solid,
  more massive,
More real; toward evening, flooded in warm light
  they disclose
Themselves colorful in deceptive proximity, proffering
Their crags and woods and villages in the golden light.
Now, in the morning, only the strong lines of the ridges
And summits are visible, those in front blue-gray,
  those behind

Immer lichter und dünner und silberner: aber die Augen
Wenden sich bald von dem blendenden Blick in den Ost
    und beginnen
Alsbald ihr Tagwerk am Boden, des Gartens Herren
    und Wächter.
Hier erspähn sie im Erdbeergeschoß das junge Geranke,
Da und dort auch dazwischen ein Unkraut, nah schon
    am Blühen,
Das man am besten sogleich wegnimmt, eh es Zeit hat,
    die Blüte
Auszubilden und rings zu verstreun den unzähligen Samen.
Auch der Fußweg, der schmale, im Zickzack dem
    Berg eingeschnitten,
Fordert zuweilen Beachtung, weckt Sorgen oder macht Freude,
Je nachdem er sich hielt im letzten Regenguß: ob er
Brävlich die Wasser entließ ins Gras durch die
    seitlichen Rinnen,
Oder ob er—auch dies erlebt ich des öftern—vor Schrecken
Einem Gewitterguß die gefährdeten Böschungen preisgab,
Daß Gerölle und Sand im Grase sich stauen, indessen
Tief das Weglein gespalten aufklafft in schartigen Rissen.
Hier in den schmalen Nebenterrassen ist außer dem Weinstock
Wenig gepflanzt, es ist zu steil und zu weit weg vom Wasser
Oder zu sehr von den Reben verschattet; immerhin sucht man
Auch diesem schwierigen Land noch abzugewinnen
    ein Kleines:
Niedere Bohnen etwa, Erdbeeren, auch Kohl oder Erbsen.
Hier auch hat, auf der besten und breitsten Terrasse,
    ihr Pflanzland
Natalina, die hochverdiente, die viele Jahre mir treu war,

Luminous, always brighter and thinner, more silver:
    but my eyes
Soon turn from the dazzling sight in the east and as soon start
Their day's work on the ground, masters and keepers of
    the garden.
In the strawberry patch they detect a young tangle of runners;
Or, here and there, a weed about to bloom, which at best
Can be pulled up before the flower has had time to
Develop and broadcast its innumerable seeds.
The narrow footpath, cut into the hill in a zigzag,
Sometimes requires attention, wakes care or brings joy,
Depending on how it weathered the last downpour:
    if it bravely
Let the waters into the grass through the lateral channels,
Or if—and this I've seen more often—out of fear it
Surrendered the vulnerable slopes to a sudden downpour,
So that rubble and sand pile up in the grass, while
The little path, deeply cleft, tears open in jagged rifts.
In the meager terrace close by, besides grapevines little
Is planted; it's too steep and too far from the water, and
Gets too much shade from the vines; nonetheless one still tries
To win a little something from this difficult land:
Beans that grow close to the ground, strawberries, cabbage
    or peas.
Here too, on the best and broadest terrace, Natalina
    plants:
Most worthy Natalina, for many years a loyal servant,

Seit sie im Ruhestand lebt und nicht mehr die
    Küche verwaltet.
Und sie besorgt es treulich, im blechernen Kesselchen
    schleppt sie
Mist von Kaninchen herbei und Asche, den Boden zu düngen.
Aber da, wo der Weg jeweils den Beeten sich nähert,
Haben wir jedes Jahr ein paar Blumen stehen, denn täglich
Geht man den Weg ja, den steilen, gar oft, und wenn
    auch die Bohnen,
Wenn auch Erbsen und Kohl vielleicht schon braun und
    versengt stehn,
Immer bekommen doch noch die paar Blumen am Rande
    ihr Wasser,
Zinnien, rotviolett, oder Löwenmaul und Kapuziner.
Ihnen vorbei, deren Frische den lechzenden
    Abhang erheitert,
Steig ich vollends zum Stalle hinab; er ist zwar
    kein Stall mehr,
War es jedoch voreinstmals und heißt noch so. Seine Tiefe,
Selten geöffnet, birgt Kisten und Flaschen und
    manches Gerümpel,
Drüber im luftigen Bodenraum lagert der Vorrat an Holze,
Brennholz sowohl für den Ofen wie Stangen und Pfähle.
    Ein Schuppen
Nebenan Obdach gewähret dem mancherlei
    Werkzeug Lorenzos,
Der die Reben besorgt, sie schneidet und bindet im Frühling
Und im Sommer sie spritzt und schwefelt, im Spätherbst
    aber und Winter
Ihnen den Kuhmist zuträgt, den sie verlangen. Der Stall ist

Who, since retiring, no longer takes charge of
     the kitchen.
Faithfully she tills the soil, in small tin pails drags
Rabbit droppings and ashes for manuring the ground.
But over there, where at times the path approaches the beds,
Each year we let a few flowers grow, because we take that
Steep path quite often, in fact every day, and when the beans
And the peas and the cabbage are already brown and scorched,
At the edge of the path a few flowers still get their water:
Red-violet zinnias, or snapdragons and nasturtiums.
Past them, whose freshness brightens the languishing slope,
     I walk
All the way down to the stable; it no longer serves that
Function, but it once did and still bears that name. Its depths,
Seldom unsealed, house boxes and bottles and all kinds
     of clutter;
Above, in the airy attic, the wood supply is kept:
Firewood for the stove, stakes and poles for the garden.
A nearby shed shelters Lorenzo's various tools;
He tends the vines, cuts and binds them in spring, waters and
Sprays them with sulphur in summer, in late autumn
     and winter
He fertilizes them with cow manure. The stable is

Treffpunkt und Mitte des Gartens. Hier dehnt sich
    ein Stück weit
Ebener Boden, ein seltenes Gut in so steilem Gelände,
Wo jedem Baum, jeder Rebe der Standort nur
    künstlich und listig
In Terrassen dem Hang abgeschmeichelt wird. Hier aber
    liegt uns,
Klein zwar und schmal, ein Riemen, doch immerhin:
    ebenen Grundes
Ein willkommenes Stück; hier ziehn wir unsre Gemüse,
Hier verbringen wir, Mann wie Weib, einen Teil unsrer Tage,
Weit vom Hause, verborgen im Grün, und wir lieben
    dies Pflanzland
Sehr, denn wahrlich es ist hier an Wert und Vorteil
    nicht wenig
Angehäuft, das der Fremde (man würdigt des Anblicks
    nicht jeden)
Kaum erkennt, aber uns ist's bekannt und wir
    schätzen es dankbar.

Zwar an Pracht und Bedeutung ist diese Terrasse beim Stalle
Nicht jener obersten gleich, wo das Haus prangt, wo
    herrlich die Aussicht
In die Weite des Seetals reicht und nach Norden ins
    hohe Gebirge,
Wo die Rosen stehn und der Buchs den Platz umsäumt,
    wo die Gäste
Rühmend die Lage des Hauses besprechen und wissen wollen,
    wie dieser

The center around which the garden revolves. Here
    a broad tract
Of level ground stretches, unusually good in such
    steep terrain,
Where every tree, every vine in the terrace of the slope
Wins its station through cunning, artifice and cajolery.
But for us this strip of level ground, albeit small and narrow,
Is a godsend; we grow our vegetables here. Far from
    the house,
Hidden in verdure, here we spend, man and wife, a portion
Of our days; truly, no little merit and gain accumulate
Here (this perception is not vouchsafed to all); though
    the stranger
Can scarcely see why, we dearly love this strip of arable
Land, knowing its importance, and we prize it with thanks.

For splendor and importance, this terrace by the stable is
No match for the higher one, from which the house sparkles
    and the view
Grandly sweeps to the distant lake valley, and northward
    into high
Mountains; and you can see the roses, and the boxwood
    hemming
The plaza; and guests, praising the site of the house, want
    to know

Gipfel genannt wird und jener . . . Nein, hier beim Stalle
     ist's anders,
Hier, Freund, schwebst du nicht hoch, ein Herr über
     Seetal und Ferne,
Blickst nicht «beinah bis Porlezza» und lauschst dem
     Entzücken der Gäste,
Hier ist bäurisches Land, wo statt Palastes der Stall steht,
Dessen östliche Wand, von Rose und Rebe bewachsen,
Auch eine köstliche Birne beschirmt, sie reift im Oktober.
Zu ihren Füßen lachen verstreut ein paar Blumen auch; häufig
Sonnt sich hier die Smaragdeidechse und bläht ihren blauen
Pfauhals wollüstig im Licht. Daneben, der Südwand des Stalles
Angeschmiegt, lagert der alte Kompost vom
     vorvorigen Jahre,
Dunkle, lockere Erde, ein Schatz, und um ihn zu schmücken,
Hab ich alljährlich auf ihm ein paar Sonnenblumen.
     Sie neigen
Schwer überm windgebogenen Stamm die Häupter, sie nähren
Sich von der köstlichen Erde und nähren sie wieder,
     verwesend,
Wenn sie im Herbst, von den Vögeln entsamt und
     geknickt von den Stürmen,
Ihre einst geilen und gierigen Leiber so müd und ergeben
Senken, der wartenden Erde und neuem
     Kreislauf entgegen.
Wunderlich ist's mit Gewächsen und Blumen, welchen
     bestimmt ist,
Innerhalb eines einzigen Jahres, ja weniger Monde,
Alle Stufen des Lebens zu gehen vom Keim bis zum Tode!

The name of this or that peak . . . No, here by the stable
    it's different:
You don't soar on high, master of the valley and the
    distance, or
Gaze "all the way to Porlezza," or listen to elated guests;
This is peasant land; in place of a palace is the stable,
Whose eastern wall, overgrown with roses and grapevines,
Shelters an exquisite pear tree that ripens in October.
At your feet, a few flowers laugh distracted; and often
The green lizard basks in the sun, lustily distending its
Blue peacock-throat. Close by, nestled against the stable's
Southern wall, is the compost heap from the year before last:
Dark, porous earth, a treasure; each year I adorn it
With sunflowers. Their heads bow heavy over their wind-bent
Stems; nourished by the precious soil, they nourish it
Anew, decomposing, when in autumn, seeded by birds,
Bent by violent storms, they sink their once sensuous
And eager bodies, so tired and submissive, toward
The waiting soil and a new cycle of seasons.
Isn't it strange how plants and flowers, in the space of
A single year, or even fewer moons, as allotted,
Go through the stages of life, from seed all the way to death!

Frühlings betrachten wir sie, wie man Kinder
    betrachtet, belustigt
Schaun wir ihr hastiges Wachsen, die dümmlichen
    Blumengesichter,
Rührend und drollig, unschuldig zugleich und gierig—
    und plötzlich
Eines Tages im späteren Sommer erscheint uns dieselbe
Blume, die uns noch eben ein Kind schien, rätselhaft anders,
Scheint uns geheimnisbeladen, uralt und müde, und dennoch
Lächelt sie, wunderbar reif, überlegen, ein mahnendes Vorbild.
Hier also leuchten die goldenen Häupter der Sonnenblumen,
    auch weiter
Jenseits des Weges im Garten erhebt sich aus der Gemüse
Niederem Wuchs noch manche, wie sie der Zufall gesät hat,
Alle konnten nicht bleiben, doch füttert und schont
    man sie gern ja.
Doch zuvörderst nun achte des Schatzes, den hier
    wir besitzen:
Neben dem Stalle am Weg, dem reinlichen, steinebestreuten,
Öffnet sich unter dem hölzernen Deckel ein weiter und tiefer
Wasserbehälter, gespeist aus einer benachbarten Quelle,
Welche auch, nahe dem Wald, die Weiden tränkt und
    des Nußbaums
Fuß befeuchtet. Das Volk von Montagnola will wissen,
Unser Quell sei besonderer Art, kalt nämlich im Sommer,
Aber des Winters lauwarm, dem Gras und den Menschen
    ein Labsal.
Diesen Wasserbehälter, durch Röhren der Quelle verbunden,
Haben, nächst einem zweiten, entfernteren, wir erst errichtet,
Während in früherer Zeit der Quell im grasigen Abhang

In spring we watch them as we watch small children, amused
By their rapid growth, their silly flower faces, touching,
Droll, innocent and greedy at the same time—when suddenly,
One day in late summer, the same flower that even now
Seemed a child, appears enigmatically other,
Secretive, age-old and tired, but smiles for all that,
Wondrously ripe, transcendent, an admonishing model.
Here the golden heads of the sunflowers gleam; farther
On, beyond the garden path, still others rise above
The low-growing vegetables, however chance has sown them;
They can't all survive, yet we feed and we tend them gladly.
But above all, pay attention to this priceless treasure:
Near the stable, on the well-kept pebbled path, beneath a
Wooden cover, a broad and deep reservoir opens. It is
Fed by a neighboring wellspring, which, near the forest,
Also waters the willow and moistens the foot of the
Nut tree. The people of Montagnola will assert
That our spring is exceptional: cool in summer, lukewarm
In winter, a tonic for the grass and for people.
In former times the spring ran down the grassy slope almost
Useless; but we built our reservoir next to another one

Beinah nutzlos zerrann. Jetzt können wir, fordert's die Hitze,
Hundert und mehr Gießkannen voll sanft
 erwärmten, gestandnen
Wassers schöpfen und reichlich dem dürstenden
Pflanzenvolk spenden.
Auch das Gemüseland hier, das ebne, ist beidseits von Reben
Eingefaßt, doch ich plane, die eine Reih, die nach Südosten
Allzuviel Sonne wegnimmt, allmählich eingehn zu lassen.
Heiter liegen gereiht, von Rebe und Pfirsich beschattet,
Eins am andern die Beete. Zwar sind von diesen Gemüsen
Nahezu alle gesät und betreut von der Frau, doch zuweilen
Seh ich auch hier ein wenig zum Rechten. Denn groß
 ist die Arbeit,
Und es hat eine Hausfrau auch außer dem Garten
 viel Pflichten,
Küche nimmt sie und Wäsche in Anspruch, es
 kommen Besuche,
Kommen geladene Gäste, oft ist's ein ermüdendes Tagwerk.
Forschend durchwandert mein Blick die stattliche
 Reihe der Beete;
Wahrlich, sie stehen nicht schlecht, auch eine geborne Bäurin
Oder Gärtnersfrau hielte sie besser kaum. Wie die Karotten
Saftig stehen und sauber! Ich schätze beim Essen sie wenig,
Aber im Garten möcht ich sie niemals missen, es wehen
Ihre laubigen Büschel so weich und duften so kernig.
Und es ernährt sich auf ihnen die grüne Raupe des edlen
Schwalbenschwanzfalters, sein Flug entzückt uns oft
 im Gelände,
Und es mahnt mich der Duft des Karottenlaubes
 der Kindheit,

And we connected it with pipes to the spring. Now we are
Able—the heat demands it—to draw a hundred or more
Cans of gently warmed, standing water and bestow it
Profusely on the thirsty generations of plants.
Even the level vegetable patch is hemmed on both sides
By grapevines; I plan to let the row toward the southeast—
It takes up too much sun—gradually wither away.
Shaded by vines and peach trees, row upon bright row
The beds lie. My wife sows and tends almost all of these
Vegetables, but at times I, too, see something here to
Set right. For the work is long, and besides, a housewife
Has many duties aside from the garden: she takes
Care of the kitchen and the washing, and sees to our
Heavy-laden guests—often an exhausting day's work.
Searching, my eyes wander through the stately rows of beds;
They don't look at all bad; a native peasant woman or
Gardener's wife could scarcely keep them better. The carrots
Look so fresh and neatly planted! I don't care for them
   at dinner,
But in the garden I'd never do without them, their leafy
Clusters sway in the breeze, so supple; their scent is so hearty.
And the green caterpillar of the noble swallowtail,
Whose flight often charms us in Ticino, feeds on their leaves.
The scent of the carrot leaves darkly recalls my childhood:

Da ich in manchem Sommer mit ihm meine
    Raupen gefüttert,
Selber mit kräftigen Zähnen die rote Rübe zerkrachend.
Ferne Jugend! Auch du wehst aus den Freuden des Gartens
In die herbstlichen Jahre mir sehnlich herüber und rührest
Oft so mahnend und herb und süß ans alternde Herz mir.
Da und dort entdeck ich ein Gras, ein fettes, das heimlich
Sich im Schatten der dichten Karotten gemästet
    und hochwuchs.
Tastend greif ich durchs Laub nach seiner
    schmarotzenden Wurzel,
Ziehe sie aus und werfe erbarmungslos in den Korb sie.
Hier ist der Petersilie Feld: Prezzemolo heißt sie
Hierzuland. Aber im Winter, wenn all die
    hier grünenden Beete
Tot und verschwunden und kalt vom Schnee des Dezembers
    bedeckt sind
Und der Pflanzen beraubt, dann steht der Prezzemolo einzig
Noch, der treue, und grünet, es schützt ihn ein Dach,
    das Lorenzo
Ihm aus Stangen erbaut und mit Reisig und
    Spargelkraut zudeckt.
Erst in diesem Jahre, nach mancher Erwägung und Sorge,
Haben wir dieses Gemüsland an zweien Stellen vergrößert,
Haben der Wiese ein paar Schritt Breite entzogen, Lorenzo
Spatete um und warf durchs Sieb die steinige Erde
Manchen Tag, es war noch halb Winter, und grub den
    nährenden Mist ein.
Eine der neuen Provinzen—Tomaten stehn dort—besuch ich
Nun zu nötiger Arbeit, ich möchte früh sie verrichten,

Many summers I would feed the leaves to my caterpillars,
Or with my own strong teeth crack the red roots to bits
        for them.
Distant youth! From the joys of the garden, you, too, blow
Ardently into my autumnal years; often so
Admonishing, acrid and sweet, you touch my aging heart.
Here and there I discover a young weed that stealthily
Fattened and grew tall in the shadow of the carrots.
Feeling through the leaves, I grasp its parasitic root,
Pull it up and mercilessly throw it into the basket.
Here is the field of parsley: *prezzemolo* they call it
In these parts. In winter, when all the beds planted here
Lie dead and gone and cold, covered by December snow,
Ravaged of plant life, then the *prezzemolo* stands alone,
Faithful, true, greening; to protect it Lorenzo built a roof
Out of poles, thatched with brushwood and asparagus fern.
Just this year, after much worry and deliberation,
We extended this vegetable patch in two places,
Thereby narrowing the meadow a few paces; Lorenzo
Spaded up the stony soil and sieved it for days—it was still
Half winter—then he plowed in the nourishing manure.
I visit one of our new provinces—planted with tomatoes—
With important work in mind; I must do this early, before

Eh der Feigenbaumschatten der steigenden Sonne
 muß weichen.
Schön in geraden Reihen, in fünfen, stehn meine Tomaten
(Meine, sag ich, denn ich bin's, der sie gepflanzt hat
 und hütet,
So wie andre Gemüse der Frau unterstehn und das
 Dasein verdanken)
Nahezu schon zu voller Höhe erwachsen, sie stehen
Saftig und strotzend im Laub, ich kann das Geheimnis
 verraten:
Jegliche Wurzel umgab ich mit feuchtem, lockerem Torfmull,
Dem ich ein Gran Kunstdünger beimischte. Probiert's!
 Es bewährt sich.
Saftig, sage ich, stehn sie im Laub, aus den knotigen Stielen
Sprießen unbändig nach allen Seiten die Blätter, und unter
 den Blättern
Da und dorten verbergen im grünen Dunkel die grünen
Jungen Früchte sich schwellend zu zweien und dreien:
 bald werden
Hochrot sie leuchten im Laub, des Sommers Erfüllung.
 Heut aber
Gilt nicht den Früchten mein Blick, er gilt vor allem
 den Stäben,
Welche den Pflanzen zur Stütze dienen. Sie stammen
Sämtlich vom nahen Walde, Kastanienstämmchen die meisten,
Doch auch Robinien sind darunter und einige
 Stämmchen von Eschen,
Mannshoch und wenig darüber, und mancher Stab ist an Höhe
Schon von der Pflanze erreicht. Denn es gibt, wie unter
 den Menschen

The shadow of the fig tree retreats from the climbing sun.
My tomatoes stand in lovely even rows of five
(Mine, I say, for I planted and tend them; just as other herbs
Are under my wife's protection and owe her their existence),
Nearly full-grown; they are succulent and swollen, in leaf.
I can reveal the secret: I surrounded their roots with
A mixture of damp, porous leaf mold and a few grains of
Artificial fertilizer. Try it! It stands the test.
Succulent, I say, they stand in leaf; from the joined stalks
Intractable leaves sprout from all sides, and under the leaves,
Hidden here and there in the green darkness, the young green
Fruits swelling in twos and threes: soon they'll be
      crimson, gleaming
In the leaves, the fulfillment of summer. But today the fruits
Don't hold my gaze; it rests, above all, on the stakes that
Support the plants. All of them come from the woods close by:
Most are chestnut saplings, but locusts, too, are among them,
And a few saplings of the ash, as tall as a man or
Somewhat taller; already the plants reach to the height
Of many of the stakes. For among plants, as among people,

Immer auch unter den Pflanzen ein paar von
    besonderer Stärke,
Gierig im Wachstum und frech und rücksichtslos gegen
    die Nachbarn,
Welche man bald, ihrer Größe wegen und Stärke, bewundert,
Bald auch in ihrem durch nichts zu stillenden
    Ehrgeiz belächelt.
Sorglich prüf ich die Stäbe, daß jeglicher fest und gerad steh,
Prüfe dann Busch um Busch die Pflanzen, das Messer
    in Händen,
Denn es gilt zu beschneiden das wilde Wachstum,
    nicht mehr als
Zwei, drei Zweige belasse ich jeder, die andern entfern ich,
Und von den zahllosen Trieben, die aus den
    Achseln der Blätter
Überall geil aufsprießen, laß ich bloß wenige stehen,
Denn es neigt dieses üppige Kraut triebhaft
    zur Vergeudung.
Schnüre sodann entnehm ich der Tasche und binde die obern
Zweige sanft an die Stäbe, da haltlos sie sind in sich selber,
Und sie wachsen so schnell, daß aller fünf Tage es nottut,
Neu sie zu binden, stets trag ich die Tasche gestopft voll
    mit Schnüren.
Andere machen's mit Bast, es ist auch hübscher für's Auge,
Mir aber war an Schnur niemals Mangel, die Bücherverleger
Senden mir täglich Pakete ins Haus, deren Schnüre
    ich sammle.
Während ich so den Tomaten aufwarte von Reihe zu Reihe,
Rückt der Vormittag vor und es sind entschwunden
    die Schatten,

A few are always particularly strong, rapacious
In growth, impudent and ruthless toward their neighbors,
But you readily admire their great size and hardiness,
And soon smile at their unappeasable ambition.
Carefully I test the stakes to see that each stands firm
      and straight,
Then bush after bush, my knife in hand, I test the plants,
For it pays to stem the wild growth: I leave no more than
Two or three branches on each, lopping off all the others;
And I leave but a few of the countless young shoots
      that sprout
Lustily from every leaf axil; for this exuberant
Plant can display a strong leaning toward profligacy.
Then, taking string from my pocket, I gently secure
The higher branches to the stakes, for the plants need support,
They grow so fast that you need to bind them every fifth
Day, and so I always stuff my pockets full of string.
Others use bast for this purpose; it's a prettier sight,
But I never lack string; I save it from the parcels
Of books publishers send to my house every day.
While I am tending the tomatoes row after row,
Morning presses on, the shadows vanish, steam rises

Schwül entdampft es dem Boden und bitter duftet
    das Blattwerk,
Das im Korb neben mir, kaum abgeschnitten, schon hinwelkt,
Und die Sonne beginnt mehr als erträglich zu stechen.
So verzieh ich mich denn, noch vor vollendeter Arbeit,
Aus dem glüh'nden Bezirk, nach Schatten begierig.
    Den find ich
Nahe dem Stall unter Maulbeerbäumen. Hier schütt ich
    den Korb aus
Auf einen Unkrautberg, der da seit langem sich anhäuft
Und in Erde zurück die zerstörten Gestaltungen wandelt.
Wohlgeschützt und verborgen ist dieser Ort unter Maulbeern,
Die mit dem festen, großblättrigen Laub ihn
    immer beschatten,
Auch ein Pfirsichbäumchen steht da, ich pflanzte es selber,
Band es am Pfahl und erhoffe noch manche Frucht
    seiner Zweige.
Unterhalb läuft die Weißdornhecke, die Grenze
    des Grundstücks,
Etwas tiefer ein Feldweg, zwar wenig begangen,
    doch manchmal
Hock ich im Grase hier oder stehe, und unter mir
    gehen die Leute,
Wähnen allein sich und ohne Zeugen, denn
    niemand vermöchte
Mich zu erspähn, und sie reden vertraulich, etwa
    zwei Weiber,
Welche zum Reisigsammeln den Wald nach
    stürmischen Nächten
Früh aufsuchen, sie gehn in den schweren bäurischen Schuhen

From the sultry ground; in the basket beside me, the leaves,
Newly cut but already withered, give off a bitter scent;
And now the sun begins to scorch rather intolerably.
Though my work's still not finished, I withdraw from
      the glowing
Region, eager for shade. I find it under the mulberry
Trees, near the stable. Here I empty my basket onto
A mountain of weeds that's been stacking up a long time,
And the demolished forms return to, turn back into earth.
This spot is well protected and concealed by the mulberries,
Whose dense, large-leafed foliage keeps it in perpetual shade;
A peach tree stands here too, I planted it myself, tied it
To a pole and still expect many fruits from its branches.
Below, marking the limit of this tract, the hawthorn
      hedge runs,
Somewhat farther down, a meadow path, little used.
      Sometimes
I crouch or stand here in the grass and watch the
      people walking
Below, who think themselves alone and unobserved, for no one
Would be able to see me; and they talk intimately,
Two women perhaps, who, after stormy nights, are out early
Gathering brushwood; slowly they walk by in their heavy

Langsam vorüber, den Tragkorb am Rücken, bleiben
    oft stehen,
Schwatzen, lachen und klagen, erzählen dieses und jenes.
Vieles vernehm ich genau, die übrige Rede geht mählich
Gegen's Gehölz hin verloren, bis nur noch das
    trockene Knacken
Der gebrochenen Äste herübertönt. Manchmal auch hör ich,
Und ich sag es nicht weiter, gedämpfte Hiebe des Gertels
In lebendiges Holz: da macht sich, tückisch bewaffnet,
Eine die Morgenstille zu nutze und haut verbotenerweise
Diesen und jenen Ast und vielleicht auch ein Stämmlein,
    ein junges,
Ihren Vorrat zu mehren . . . Dich preise ich, grünes
    Versteck du,
Unkrautgebirge im Schatten der Bäume, freundliche Zuflucht
Mancher Stunde, wenn ringsum die Sommerhitze sich austobt
Und auch die Vögel des Waldes verstummt sind, oder
    vom Zimmer
Mich ein Unmut vertrieb oder Leid, ein Mißglücken
    der Arbeit,
Eines bösen Menschen gehässiger Brief, ein Versagen
    des Mutes.
Oh, und immer hast du gleich heiter und gut mich empfangen,
Oft mich Stunden beherbergt vollkommener, göttlicher Stille,
Kaum daß etwa vom Wald ein Specht war zu hören.
    Ich danke
Manchen Traum und Gedanken dir, mancherlei
    Glück der Versenkung.
Manchmal, wenn ich hier weile, halb müßig, halb fleißig,
    kommt lautlos

Peasant shoes, baskets on their backs; often they
    stand chatting,
Laughing and complaining, talking about this and that.
I can clearly make out much of their talk, but the rest trails
Off, lost in the woods, until once again only the dry
Cracking of broken boughs resounds to where I am.
    Sometimes
I hear, and I'll say no more of this, the muffled stroke
Of the switch in the living wood: where someone, artfully
Armed, violates the morning stillness, hewing a branch
And maybe a young sapling here and there, to increase
His supply . . . I praise you, green covert, mountain of weeds
In the shade of the trees, friendly refuge of many hours,
While on all sides the summer heat vents its rage, and
    the woodland
Birds keep silence; or when moodiness or an injury
Drives me from my room: something wrong in my work,
    a spiteful
Letter from a vicious person, a failure of courage.
You have always received me heartily and well, often you've
Harbored me for hours of complete, divine silence, when one
Can scarcely hear a woodpecker in the forest. I thank you
For dreams and ideas, for the joy that comes of contemplation.
At times, while I rest here both idle and diligent, a lion

Durch die Dschungel des Gartens und Weinbergs
    Löwe gegangen,
Unser Kater, mein Freund, mein Brüderchen. Zärtlich
    miaut er,
Reibt den gesenkten Kopf an mir, blickt flehend, und wirft sich
Mit gelösten Gliedern zu Boden, zeigt Bauch mir und Kehle,
Die er stets schneeweiß trägt, und fordert zum Spielen
    heraus mich.
Öfter auch springt er, genauestens zielend, mir rasch
    auf die Schultern,
Schmiegt sich an und verweilt, sanft schnurrend, bis er
    genug hat.
Andere Male grüßt er nur kurz im stillen Vorbeischlich,
Ist gedankenvoll, hat im Walde zu tun, und verschwindet
Mit dem vornehmen Gang, der Siamesin Sohn, unser Löwe.
Ihm lebt auch noch ein Bruder, ein ehmals unendlich geliebter,
Tiger genannt, der an Kehle und Bauch von
    gelblichem Braun ist,
Aber die zärtlichen einst, die unzertrennlichen Brüder,
Einer Schüssel und eines Lagers Genossen vor Zeiten,
Leben in bittrer Feindschaft heut, seit mit dem
    Hinwelken der Kindheit
Männerleidenschaft sie und Männereifersucht trennte.

Jetzt auch flücht ich hierher, den Nacken glüh'nd
    von der Sonne,
Müde im Rücken, die Augen verwelkt, und will
    bis zum Mittag
Hier bei spielerisch mühlosem Tun mich erholen und weilen.

Soundlessly walks through the jungle of garden and vineyard,
Our cat, my friend, my little brother. He meows tenderly,
Rubs his lowered head against me, looks imploring and
Nimbly throws himself to the ground, shows me
            his snow-white
Belly and neck, demands that I play with him. More often,
Aiming precisely, quickly he leaps onto my shoulders,
Nestles against me and tarries until he's had enough.
Other times, prowling past in silence, he greets me curtly,
Is pensive, has something to do in the woods, disappears
With his aristocratic gait, son of the Siamese,
Our lion. His brother—once infinitely beloved—Tiger,
Whose neck and belly are yellowish brown, is still alive;
But the once affectionate, the inseparable
Brothers, former companions of bowl and lair, now live
In bitter enmity, since with the fading of childhood
Male passion and male jealousy parted them.

Now I, too, take refuge here, my neck red-hot from the sun,
My back tired, my eyelids drooping, and until noon I want
To rest and relax in playful, effortless occupation.

Vorher hol ich im Schuppen ein kleines
    handliches Rundsieb,
Hole auch Feuerzeug und Papiers eine Handvoll, denn selten
Halt ich an diesem Orte mich auf, ohne Feuer zu zünden.
Mancherlei Herkunft und Wurzel hat wohl diese
    Neigung zum Feuern,
Von der knäbischen Lust an Zündeln bis rückwärts
    zum Opfer
Abels oder des Abraham, denn jede Gewohnheit,
    sei's Tugend,
Sei es Laster, ist ja bis tief in die Vorwelt verwurzelt,
Hat aber jedem Einzelnen ihren besonderen Sinn doch.
Mir zum Beispiel bedeutet das Feuer (nebst Vielem,
    das es bedeutet)
Auch einen chymisch-symbolischen Kult im Dienste
    der Gottheit,
Heißt mir Rückverwandlung der Vielfalt ins Eine, und ich bin
Priester dabei und Diener, vollziehe und werde vollzogen,
Wandle das Holz und Kraut zu Asche, helfe dem Toten
Rascher entwerden und sich entsühnen, und geh in mir selber
Oftmals dabei meditierend dieselben sühnenden Schritte
Rückwärts vom Vielen ins Eine, der Gottesbetrachtung
    ergeben.
So vollzog Alchymie die Prozesse und Opfer des Läuterns
Einst am Metall überm Feuer, erhitzte es, ließ es erkalten,
Gab Chemikalien zu und harrte auf Neumond und Vollmond,
Und indes am Metall sich vollzog die göttliche Wandlung,
Die es zum edelsten Gute, zum Stein der Weisen veredelt,
Tat der fromme Adept im eigenen Herzen dasselbe,
Sublimierte und läuterte sich, vollzog die Prozesse

I usually fetch a small, handy, round sieve from the shed,
Along with a handful of papers and matches, for I seldom
Stop at this place without lighting a fire. This fascination
With fire probably has a multiple origin and root—
From the boyish bent to play with it, back to the sacrifice
Of Abel or Abraham; for every custom, be it virtue,
Be it vice, is deeply rooted in former ages, though
A custom has its own special meaning for each person.
To me, for example, fire signifies (besides much else)
A chymic-symbolic cult in the service of the godhead:
The reconversion of the Many into the One.
I am its priest and servant; I fulfill and become fulfilled,
Changing the wood and plants to ashes, helping the dead be
Sooner at home, absolved; meditating, I often go into
Myself, take those same atoning steps backward
          from the Many
To the One, given over to the beatific vision.
So alchemy once accomplished the process and sacrifice of
Purification: The metal was heated over fire, left to cool,
Chemicals were added, the new and full moons awaited;
While the divine transformation took place in the metal,
Ennobling it to the greatest good, the philosopher's stone,
In his heart the pious adept did the same: sublimated
And purified himself, himself completing the process

Chemischer Wandlung in sich, meditierend,
    wachend und fastend,
Bis am Ende der Übung, nach Tagen oder nach Wochen,
Gleich dem Metalle im Tiegel auch seine Seele entgiftet,
Seine Sinne geläutert und er bereit war zur
    mystischen Einung.
Nun, ich sehe euch lächeln, o Freunde, und wohl mögt
    ihr lächeln,
Daß mein Kauern und Schüren am Boden, mein Zündeln
    und Köhlern,
Meine kindliche Lust am einsamen Träumen und Brüten
So sich mit Gleichnissen schmücke, ja brüste. Indessen,
    ihr Lieben,
Wisset ihr, wie es gemeint ist, und wie ich ja all
    mein Dichten verstehe,
Als Beschönigung nicht, als Bekenntnis nur, und ihr duldet
Also mein Phantasieren . . . Ich kauere also im Schatten
Zwischen dem Unkrautberg und der Hecke, reibe
    das Zündholz,
Lasse Papier aufflammen und leg ein paar Halme
    und Blätter
Lose darüber, dann mehr, erst Trocknes nur, schließlich
    auch Grünes.
Später, im Herbste, lieb ich das offne, flammende Feuer,
Jetzt aber, wegen der Wärme und auch aus
    Mangel an Holze
(Welches dann später die Stürme der Äquinoktien liefern),
Streb ich danach, ein bedecktes, ein still in sich
    glosendes Feuer,
Einen ruhig rauchenden Meiler zu pflegen, der halbe

Of chemical change, meditating, keeping watch and fasting;
Until, at the end of the exercise, after days or weeks,
Like the metal in the crucible, his own soul became pure,
His senses cleansed; he was ready for mystical union.
Now I see you are smiling, my friends, and well you may smile
At my crouching, my poking, playing with fire,
        charcoal-burning,
My childish need to embellish my lonely dreams and broodings
With parables, even boasting of them. All the while,
        dear friends,
You understand my meanings, as I my musing, not as
Embellishment, but only as avowal; and so you will
Humor my indulgence in reveries . . . Between the mountain
Of weeds and the hedge, I crouch in the shade, strike
        a match,
Let the paper catch fire and scatter a few straws and
        leaves on it,
Then feed it, first with dry twigs, finally with green as well.
Later on, in autumn, I love an open flaming fire,
But now, because of the extreme heat and for lack of wood
(Which the equinoctial storms later will supply),
I light a stack of brushwood layered with earth, nurse
        a covered
Fire that will glow in itself, smoldering gently for half

Oder auch ganze Tage leis fortglimmt. Drum nennt mich
    auch «Köhler»
Oft meine Gattin, des Rauchgeruchs wegen und wohl auch
Meiner Neigung wegen zum Glauben, sie teilet ihn selber
Nicht und duldet ihn doch an mir, und mit mehr als
Bloßer Geduld, ich will ihrer dafür im Rauchopfer
    gedenken,
Die heut außer dem Haus weilt, im Tal, in der Stadt,
    in Lugano.
Noch einen Köhlerglauben, noch einen von vielen, bekenn ich:
Daß ich vom Erdebrennen viel halte; man übt es,
    so scheint mir,
Heute nicht mehr, die Chemie hat andere Mittel gefunden,
Erde zu bessern, zu läutern, zu fetten oder entsäuern,
Auch hat niemand mehr Zeit in unsern Tagen, zu sitzen
Und sich Erden zu brennen am Feuer—wer zahlte
    den Taglohn?
Ich aber bin ein Dichter und zahl es mit
    mancher Entbehrung,
Manchem Opfer vielleicht, dafür hat Gott mir gestattet,
Nicht bloß in unseren Tagen zu leben, sondern der Zeit mich
Oft zu entschlagen und zeitlos zu atmen im Raume,
    einst galt das
Viel und wurde Entrückung genannt oder
    göttlicher Wahnsinn.
Heute gilt es nichts mehr, weil heute so kostbar
    die Zeit scheint,
Zeitverachtung aber ein Laster sei. «Introversion» heißt
Bei den Spezialisten der Zustand, von dem ich hier spreche,

Or a whole day. On this account, my wife often calls me
"The charcoal-burner": because of the smell of smoke,
        and perhaps,
Too, because she herself does not share this faith of mine,
Though she tolerates it in me with more than mere patience;
Today I want to remember her in my smoke offering,
While she lingers in the valley, in the city, in Lugano.
One more blind faith, one more among many, I profess:
I think highly of burning earth: this practice seems to
Have died out; chemistry has found other means of improving,
Purifying, enriching and sweetening the soil;
And, nowadays, no one has the time any more to sit
And burn soil over a fire—who would pay the wages?
As a poet I pay with much self-denial, perhaps
Many sacrifices; thus God has permitted me
To live not only in these days, but often has stripped me
Of time, and timeless let me breathe in space; once this was
Precious, people called it rapture or divine madness.
In our time it's worthless, since today time seems so precious
And contempt for it would be a vice. Specialists have
A term for the condition I speak of, "introversion,"

Und bezeichnet das Tun eines Schwächlings, der sich
    den Pflichten
Seines Lebens entzieht und im Selbstgenuß seiner Träume
Sich verliert und verspielt und den kein Erwachsener
    ernst nimmt.
Nun, so werden von Menschen und Zeiten
    die Güter verschieden
Eingeschätzt, und es sei mit dem Seinen ein jeder zufrieden.
Aber zurück zur Erde! Ich sprach vom Brennen
    und Köhlern,
Das ich so gern betreibe und das heut nicht mehr
    modern ist.
Einstmals herrschte der Glaube, man könne durch Brennen
    die Erde
Heilsam erneuern und fruchtbar machen, zum Beispiel
    bei Stifter,
Einem Dichter, von dem ich viel halte, «brennen»
    die Gärtner
Sich verschiedene Erden, und so versuche auch ich es.
Aus dem Abfall, dem Grünzeug, den Wurzeln,
    die ich verbrenne,
Alle mit Erde gemischt, entstehet teils dunkle, teils helle,
Rötliche teils, teils graue Asche, sie lagert am Grunde
Meiner Feuerstelle, so fein wie das feinste
    Mehl oder Pulver.
Diese dann, peinlich gesiebt, bedeutet den Stein mir
    der Weisen,
Ist mir Ertrag und köstliche Frucht der
    verköhlerten Stunden,

Denoting the actions of a weakling who shuns life's
Duties, losing himself, losing all in gratifying
His own dreams, and whom no adult can take seriously.
Now, people and the times will place different values
On goods, so let everyone be satisfied with his own.
But back to the earth! I spoke of burning and
      charcoal-burning,
Which I so love to do, and which is now unfashionable.
Once the belief was widespread that, through burning, the soil
Could be restored and made fertile; you find this, for instance,
In Stifter—a poet I highly esteem—gardeners
"Burn" different soils, and so I, too, attempt this.
I make a thorough mixture of earth, refuse, herbs and roots,
And burn them; their ashes, partly dark, part light,
      partly reddish,
Partly gray, pile up on the floor of my hearth, as fine
As the finest flour or powder. These ashes, sieved
Painstakingly, are my philosopher's stone, the return
And precious fruit of many charred hours. I carry them off

Die ich in kleinem Kessel wegtrage und sparsam im
      Garten verteile,
Nur die geliebteren Blumen und etwa das Gärtchen der Gattin
Würdige ich eines Anteils an diesem sublimen Erträgnis
Meditativer Feuer und Opfer. Auch heute bedeck ich,
Kauernd wie ein Chinese, den Strohhut tief über den Augen,
Sorgsam die schwelende Glut abwechselnd mit Trocknem
      und Feuchtem,
Und es geht mir noch einmal das ganze Zeug durch
      die Hände,
Das ich hier angesammelt auf großem Haufen. Da liegen
Alle Arten von Kraut und Unkraut, Schmarotzer der Beete,
Liegt geschoßner Salat und Gurkengrün und dazwischen
Oft noch ein Stäbchen aus Holz mit drein
      geklemmtem Papierchen,
Zeichen einst, daß ein Beet in Hoffnung mit Samen bestellt sei,
Unnütz längst, überholt, so wie die Weisheit der Alten
Und der Heiligen Schrift heut überholt ist und mancher
Sie mit den Füßen tritt und belacht gleich diesem Haufen
      von Abfall.
Dem Besinnlichen aber, dem Müßiggänger und Träumer,
Dem Empfindsamen sind sie wertvoll, ja heilig, wie alles,
Was das Menschengemüt in Betrachtung und
      Denken beruhigt,
Daß es der Leidenschaften und Triebe besonnener Herr wird.
Aber auch jene Leidenschaft, jene heftige Lust muß
      man zähmen,
Welche die andern verbessern, die Welt erziehen, Geschichte
Aus Ideen gestalten will, denn es ist leider die Welt nun
So beschaffen, daß dieser Trieb edlerer Geister, wie alle

In a small pail and sparingly disperse them in the garden;
Only the better-loved flowers and my wife's little garden
Are vouchsafed a portion of this sublime produce of
Meditative fire and sacrifice. And today,
Crouching like a Chinaman, my straw hat low over
My eyes, I carefully lay dry and moist things alternately
On the fire. Once again everything I've gathered into
This great heap, the whole substance passes through
     my hands:
Every species of plant and weed, parasites of the beds,
Tough lettuce leaves, cucumber vines, often among them
A small wooden stake with a slip of paper attached—
Once a sign that a bed was sown and tilled in hope, long since
Useless, out of date, just as the wisdom of the ages and
The Holy Scriptures are now out of date. Many have
Trampled them and ridiculed them like this refuse pile.
But to the contemplative, the indolent, the dreamer,
To the sensitive they are precious, yes, sacred as all
That soothes the human spirit through thought and
     contemplation,
Making it the prudent master of passion and impulse.
But even that passion, that vehement desire that improves
Others, civilizes the world, that will shape history
From ideas, must be tamed; for unfortunately the world
Is now such that this instinct of nobler spirits, like all

Andern Triebe am Ende zu Blut und Gewalttat und
    Krieg führt,
Und das Weisesein bleibt Alchymie und Spiel für die Weisen,
Während die Welt von rohern, doch heftigern Trieben
    regiert wird.
Also bescheiden wir uns, und setzen wir möglichst
    dem Weltlauf
Auch in drangvoller Zeit jene Ruhe der Seele entgegen,
Welche die Alten gerühmt und erstrebt, und tun wir das Gute.
Ohne an Ändrung der Welt gleich zu denken; auch so wird
    sich's lohnen.

Ringsum schweigt und lastet der heiße Mittag, kein Laut ist
In den Lüften als fern und tief auf der Straße im Tale
Etwa ein Wagenrollen und manchmal ein Knistern im Feuer,
Wenn der Brand eine Wurzel durchdörrt hat und
    gierig verzehret.
Ruhend, doch nie ganz müßig, knie ich am Boden und fülle
Sanft mit den Händen das schön gerundete Sieb
    mit der Asche,
Die noch von früheren Feuern stammt, und mische
    Erde dazwischen,
Alte, warmfeuchte, vom Grund des Haufens, durchzogen
Leise von Gärung und Moder, und schüttle das
    lockre Gemische
Sachte, daß unter dem Siebe ein kleiner Kegel heranwächst
Feinster aschiger Erde. Und ohne zu wollen, verfall ich
So beim Schütteln in feste, einander gleichende Takte.
Aus dem Takt wiederum erchafft die nie müde Erinnrung

Other instincts, in the end leads to bloodshed,
      outrage and war;
While the world is ruled by coarser, yet more violent forces,
Wisdom remains alchemy and diversion for the wise.
And so, let us be modest, even in an age of oppression
Let us set against the course of the world that calm of the soul
The old ones praised and aspired to, let us do good.
Without a thought of changing the world, even so it will pay.

Around me the noon heat is hushed and heavy, not a sound
In the breeze, except, perhaps, wheels rolling on a road
Far off, deep in the valley; or a crackling in the fire
When the flames have dried out and greedily eaten a root.
Pausing, though not wholly idle, I kneel on the ground, with
Both hands gently fill the handsome, round sieve with ashes
From previous fires; I mix soil in with them; old, warm,
Moist soil from the bottom of the heap, lightly blended
With ferment and leaf mold; I shake the porous mixture
Slowly, so that under the sieve a small cone grows upward,
A cone of finest, ashen earth. Against my will, I fall
Into the rhythm of my sifting, we mark the same time.
From the beat, memory, never tired, again constructs

Eine Musik, ich summe sie mit, noch ohne mit Namen
Sie und mit Autor zu kennen, dann weiß ich es plötzlich:
     von Mozart
Ist's ein Quartett mit Oboe . . . Und nun beginnt
     im Gemüt mir
Ein Gedankenspiel, dessen ich mich schon seit Jahren befleiße,
Glasperlenspiel genannt, eine hübsche Erfindung,
Deren Gerüst die Musik und deren Grund Meditation ist.
Josef Knecht ist der Meister, dem ich das Wissen um diese
Schöne Imagination verdanke. In Zeiten der Freude
Ist sie mir Spiel und Glück, in Zeiten des Leids
     und der Wirren
Ist sie mir Trost und Besinnung, und hier am Feuer,
     beim Siebe,
Spiel ich es oft, das Glasperlenspiel, wenn auch längst noch
     wie Knecht nicht.
Während der Kegel sich türmt und vom Siebe das Erdmehl
     herabrinnt,
Während mechanisch dazwischen, sobald es nötig, die Rechte
Meinen rauchenden Meiler bedient oder neu mit Erde
     das Sieb füllt,
Während vom Stall her die großen Blumensonnen
     mich anschaun
Und hinterm Rebengezweig die Ferne mittagsblau duftet,
Hör ich Musik und sehe vergangne und künftige Menschen,
Sehe Weise und Dichter und Forscher und Künstler einmütig
Bauen am hunderttorigen Dom des Geistes—ich will es
Einmal später beschreiben, noch ist der Tag nicht gekommen.
Aber er komme nun früh oder spät oder komme
     auch niemals,

A piece of music; I hum along, still without knowing
Its name or author; suddenly it strikes me: an oboe
Quartet by Mozart . . . Within me, my thoughts begin to play
A game, an exercise I have practiced for many years,
It is called the Glass Bead Game, a charming invention
Whose framework is music, whose basis is meditation.
Joseph Knecht is the Master to whom I owe my knowledge
Of this lovely fantasia. In happy times it's a game
That delights me; in troubled times it is consolation,
Helping me reflect; here by the fire, by the sieve I often
Play the Glass Bead Game, though not yet nearly as well
          as Knecht.
While the cone towers up and the earth-meal runs out
          of the sieve,
And, as soon as required, my right hand mechanically
Tends the smoking stack or again fills the sieve with
          fresh earth,
While from the stable the tall flower-suns hold me
          in their gaze,
And behind the tangle of grapevines the distance smells
          noon-blue,
I hear music and see men of the past and the future,
Wise men and poets and scholars and artists, all of one mind,
Building the hundred-gated cathedral of the spirit—I
Will describe this at some later time, its day has not yet come.
But it will come, sooner or later, or may never come.

Immer wird mich, so oft ich des Trostes bedarf,
　　Josef Knechtens
Freundlich sinnvolles Spiel, den alten Morgenlandfahrer,
Aus den Zeiten und Zahlen entrücken zu göttlichen Brüdern,
Deren harmonischer Chor auch meine Stimme mit aufnimmt.

Horch, da weckt mich, nachdem eine Stunde, nachdem
　　eine kleine
Ewigkeit sanft mich gewiegt, eine frische Stimme. Vom Hause
Ruft mir, von Stadt und Einkauf zurückgekommen,
　　die Gattin,
Und ich rufe zurück und erhebe mich, lege die letzten
Hände voll roher Materie auf mein alchymisches Feuer,
Bringe das Sieb in den Schuppen und steige im
　　blendenden Glaste
Unseren Zickzackweg bergan zum Kiesplatz und Hause,
Sie zu begrüßen und ihr für ihre bevorzugten Blumen,
Für ihren Mohn und Zwergrittersporn, eine reichliche Gabe
Dunkelster Aschenerde als Dung zu versprechen. Und gerne
Tret ich, jetzt plötzlich die Glut und die Müdigkeit fühlend,
　　die Stufen
Vollends hinan und hinein in den kühlen
　　Schatten des Hauses,
Wasche die Hände, und schon lädt meine Frau mich zu Tische,
Schöpft die Suppe, erzählt von der Stadt und meint, es wär'
　　an der Zeit wohl,
Daß ich das nächste Mal sie dorthin begleite, die Haare
Hingen mir wieder so lang im Nacken, man müsse

Whenever I need consoling, Joseph Knecht's amiable,
Compelling game comes to me, that old man who journeyed
To the East, transported through ages and numbers to
      his divine
Brothers, whose harmonious chorus also takes in
      my own voice.

After an hour, after an eternal moment has cradled me,
Listen, a fresh voice awakens me. Back from the city,
Back from shopping, my wife calls to me from the
      house; and I
Call back and get up, lay the last handfuls of raw matter
On my alchemical fire, take the sieve to the shed,
And in the dazzling radiance I climb our zigzag path
Uphill to the broad gravel bed and the house, in order
To greet her and to promise her favorite flowers,
Her poppies and dwarf larkspur, a rich gift of darkest
Ashen earth as manure. And I step gladly,
Suddenly feeling the heat and my own tiredness,
I climb the stairs and walk into the cool shade of the house,
Wash my hands, and shortly my wife calls me to the table,
Ladles the soup, talks of the city and remarks it's
High time I went with her on her next trip into town,
My hair's got so long that it covers my neck, I must

Sie mir schneiden, ich sei ja schließlich ein Mensch und
    kein Waldgott.
    Dann erkundigt sie sich, meine Abwehr wenig beachtend,
Nach dem Garten, und bald beschäftigt uns lebhaft die Frage,
Ob es heut abend nottue, ihn ganz oder größerenteils doch
Zu begießen (es ist dies eine Arbeit für Stunden
Und nicht die leicht'ste fürwahr) oder ob von dem
    neulichen Regen
Noch etwas Feuchte geblieben sei, welches wir
    schließlich bejahen,
Um unser Mahl mit Himbeeren, den köstlichen
    roten und gelben
Von der oberen Quellenterrasse zufrieden zu enden.

1936

Get a haircut, after all I'm a man, not a satyr.
Then, scarcely noting my reluctance, she inquires about
The garden; and a lively debate ensues as to whether
We need to water all or most of it this evening
(Truly an arduous task, a labor of hours),
Or whether enough moisture has remained in the ground
From the recent rainfall—which at last we agree on,
To finish our meal with raspberries, the delicious red and
Yellow ones from the upper terrace near the spring, content.

1936

Pavillon im Winter

Urenkelstiefkind eines hadrianischen Tempels,
Illegitimer Erbe mediceischer Villen.
Mit einem Hauch Erinnerung an Versailles
Gepudert, lächelst du
Mit deinen Treppen, Säulen, Vasen und Voluten,
Unheimisch am barbarischen Strand,
Blickst in ein Land, dem du nicht angehörst,
Schickst Reize aus und Zauber,
Die nicht dein eigen sind;
Und Schnee blickt ringsum kalt
Durch deine allzuvielen Scheiben.

Du gleichst in der geliehenen Pracht
Dem armen Mädchen, das am Straßenrand
Der Großstadt steht und etwas mühsam lächelt
Und nicht so schön ist wie es scheinen will,
Und nicht so reich wie sein gefälschter Schmuck,
Und nicht so froh wie seine bunte Larve.
Ihm gleichst du; etwas Spott
Und etwas Mitleid gibt dir Antwort.
Und Schnee blickt ringsum fremd
Und kalt durch deine allzuvielen Scheiben.

Dezember 1950

54

Pavilion in Winter

❧

Stepchild, great-grandchild of one of Hadrian's temples,
Illegitimate heir of Medicean villas.
Dusted lightly with a reminder of
Versailles, you smile
With your stairways, pillars, vases, volutes,
Alien on the barbaric shore,
Gazing into a land to which you don't belong,
Exuding charm and magic
Not your own;
And all around you snow looks cold
Through your redundant panes.

For your borrowed splendor you are like
Some poor girl who stands in a doorway
In a big city and with some effort smiles:
Not so lovely as she'd like to seem,
Not so rich as her costume jewelry,
Not so cheerful as her painted face.
You're like her; a touch of scorn,
A touch of pity answer you.
And all around you snow looks strange
And cold through your redundant panes.

December 1950

Der Lahme Knabe
Eine Erinnerung aus der Kindheit

Einsam steht und verloren im Bilderbuch meiner Erinnrung
Seine blasse Gestalt, die dürftige, wunderlich fremde,
Namenlose, denn selbst den Namen mißgönnt' ihm
    sein Schicksal;
Einen Über- und Spottnamen nur, seine
    Lahmheit bezeichnend,
Gab ihm die Knabenschaft, gab ihm die Stadt, einen
    häßlichen Namen,
Den ich nicht mag überliefern, ich suche umsonst
    im Gedächtnis
Seinen wirklichen Namen. Es paßt zu des Knaben
    Erscheinung,
Daß er so namenlos blieb, ein Zwerg, ein Albe,
    ein Fremdling.
Wann ich zuerst ihn sah, wann zuletzt, ich hab es vergessen,
Aus der unendlichen Bilderflut der gesegneten Kindheit
Spülte den Fremdling mir einst eine Welle heran, eine Weile
War er mir nah, Kamerad halb, halb Lehrer, begönnert
    und Gönner,
War einen Knabensommer, zwei Knabensommer Gefährte
Meiner liebsten Tage und Freuden, und blieb mir
    so fremd doch,
Daß mit dem Sommer und Herbst er hinschwand,
    nie mehr gesehen,

The Lame Boy
A Recollection from Childhood

His pale figure stands alone in the picture book of my
Memory, lost there, spindly, singularly strange, nameless,
His own destiny failed to grant him even a name;
The other boys, the townspeople called him by a nickname
In token of his lameness, a scornful, hideous name
I don't care to pass on; in vain I search my memory
For his real name. Like a dwarf, a demon, an alien,
The boy has remained nameless. Nor can I remember
The first and last times I saw him; from blessed childhood's
Endless deluge of images a wave washed the stranger
Toward me one day, for a time he was close to me; though
Patronized, he was a comrade, a teacher, my patron,
And for one or two boyhood summers the companion
Of my happiest days and delights; yet he remained distant
And vanished with summer and autumn, never again seen

Nie mehr gesucht und begehrt, und dann plötzlich im
    wachsenden Frühling
Eines Tags, dem Vergessen enttaucht, wieder da war
    und da blieb.
Seine Gestalt zu beschwören, die in Jahrzehnten vergeßne,
Ihn noch einmal zu sehn und ihm Gruß und Dank
    zu entbieten,
Treibt es mich heut, und ich folge dem Wink des
    verborgenen Mahners,
Sinke geschlossenen Aug's in die Zeiten zurück und besinne
Aller Züge mich wieder des armen seltsamen Knaben.
Als ich ein Schüler war von zehn, elf Jahren, ein stolzer
Und begehrlicher Knabe, im Innern zwar scheu und
    voll Ehrfurcht,
Aber auch reizbar zugleich, zu erzürnen so leicht wie
    zu rühren,
Gab es im Städtchen, ein allen bekannter und
    trauriger Anblick,
Einen verwachsenen, hinkenden Knaben in
    ärmlicher Kleidung,
Der sich elend mit lahmem Beine hinschleppt', mit der Rechten
Krampfhaft auf einen Krückstock gestützt und die Linke
Stets und bei jedem Schritt auf das Knie gedrückt, seine Tritte
Klirrten in einem plump hüpfenden, mühsamen Dreitakt.
Klirrten, sag ich, denn um das lahme Bein lagen Schienen
Eng aus Eisen mit Leder geschnürt, die metallnen Gelenke
Hörte man hart sich bewegen, auch wenn das Aug
    die Maschine,
Unter dem weiten langen Beinkleid verborgen, nur unten
Überm dünnen Knöchel entdeckte. Ich kannte den Knaben,

Or sought or desired; one day in the burgeoning spring
Suddenly he emerged from oblivion, returned to stay.
Today I feel compelled to conjure up his face, forgotten
For decades, to see him once again, to greet and thank him,
And I follow the sign of the hidden admonisher,
With shut eyes sink back into those times, recollecting,
I see all the features of the poor, strange boy once again.
When I was a schoolboy, ten or eleven years old,
Proud and greedy, though inwardly shy and reverent,
But sensitive too—as easily provoked as moved—
In our town one sight was sad and familiar to all:
A misshapen, limping boy in shabby clothing, who dragged
Himself miserably along on his lame leg, his cramped
Right hand holding fast to a crutch; his left hand pressing
His left knee with every step he took, his footsteps
Clattered in awkward, erratic, laborious triple time.
Clattered, I say, for his left leg was hemmed in by narrow
Iron bands fastened with leather; you could hear the
       harsh sound
Of the metallic joints in motion, though your eye discovered
The machine—hidden beneath his long, broad trousers—only
Down below, above his thin ankle. Like everyone else,

Wie ein jeder ihn kannte, vom Sehen, es zwang mich
    die Neugier,
Halb mit Grausen gemischt, ihm oft mit den Blicken zu folgen,
Der entstellten Figur mit dem Stock, die im Gehn
    mit der Linken
Fest das linke Knie eindrückte, als dürfe es nimmer
Je sich biegen, und steif im Geklirr seiner
    Schienen enthinkte.
Mich, den Augenfrohen und Schaubegierigen, lockte
Alles Fremde, Groteske, und heimlich hatt ich nicht selten
Seine Gangart schauspielernd kopiert, bis ich
    Hände und Füße,
Beine, Knie und Schultern getreu wie er selbst zu bewegen,
So auch die Art des Gebrechens dumpf
    nachzufühlen vermochte.
Mir im Alter um ein, zwei Jahre voraus, war der Lahme
Im Gesicht so erwachsen, so alt und wissend und frühklug,
Hatte für jeden Gesunden, und so auch für mich,
    einen Blick von
Leise spöttischem Wissen, darin mehr Verachtung als Neid lag,
Daß meinem Mitleid für ihn eine heimliche Achtung
    gesellt war.

Diesen Knaben nun sah ich einstmals im Sommer alltäglich
Auf der steinernen Brücke einsam mit Angeln beschäftigt,
Manchmal umstanden von anderen oder gehänselt, es gab da
Manch überlieferten Zuruf und Witz, ich habe zum Beispiel
Hundertmal eine uralte Formel vernommen, die Warnung:

I knew him by sight; curiosity, half mixed with horror,
Often forced me to follow him with my gaze: the distorted
Figure with a crutch, who in walking clutched his left knee
So tightly it seemed that knee might never bend, and stiff
In the clanking of the iron bands, hobbled away.
Young as I was, wide-eyed and eager for new sights, all
That was strange and grotesque lured me. In secret,
      like a mime,
I had often copied his way of walking, practiced until
I could move my hands, feet, legs, knees and shoulders
      as he did,
Until I could dimly sympathize with his handicap.
The lame boy was a year or two older than I, but his face
Was so adult, old, knowing and precocious, that to each
Healthy person, and so to me, it had a look of gentle,
Mocking knowledge, in which more contempt than envy lay;
Thus my pity for him was mingled with secret respect.

I used to see this boy every day in the summer
Busy fishing all by himself on the stone bridge, sometimes
Surrounded or teased by other boys; they would shout out
Any number of trite old sayings, for example,
I heard the age-old adage a hundred times, the warning:

«Fang nur um Gottes willen den Alten nicht, denn
    sonst gibt es
Niemals Junge mehr»—und ich habe mir damals den «Alten»
Manchmal in Phantasien gemalt: einen Wels, einen Walfisch,
Ungeheuer und tausend Jahr alt, mit Moos auf dem Schädel,
Vater und König der Fische . . . Der lahme Knabe war meistens
Ganz allein, ich sah ihn mit dünnen Fingern und klugen
Griffen die Schnur auslegen, den Angelhaken mit Köder
Neu bestecken, mit Schwung auswerfen
    die feuchtblanke Leine
Oder sie sorgsam und leise ins Nagoldwasser versenken,
Das unterm Bogen der Brücke mit grünem
    Schimmer herstarrte.
Da nun auch mir ein Zug zu der Wassertiefen Geheimnis
Und zum Fischvolk und Fischfang, ich weiß nicht woher,
    im Geblüt lag,
Und ich selber schon öfter die kindischen ersten Versuche
Unternommen, den Fisch am Ufer mit Händen zu fangen
Oder am Faden von Garne, dem Nähzeug der
    Mutter entnommen,
Mit gekrümmter Stecknadel die Angel plump zu ersetzen,
Da auch ich diese Brüstung der Brücke damals nicht selten
Mir zum Jagdgebiet wählte, so ward unversehens
    der Lahme
Bald mir ein häufiger Nachbar und fast Kamerad,
    wenn auch anfangs
Der ironische Blick aus den grauen Augen, der lächelnd
Meine Garne und Haken und mich und
    mein Tun kritisierte,
Mir mißfiel und fatal war. Denn es war jener Lahme

"For God's sake don't catch the old one, or there won't be any
Young any more"—and in those days I sometimes pictured
The "old one" in my imagination: a catfish,
A whale, monstrous, a thousand years old, moss on his skull,
Father and king of the fish . . . The lame boy usually
Kept to himself; I watched his thin and skillful fingers
Grasp and give out the line, put fresh bait on the fishhook,
Cast out the shining-wet line with verve, or with great care
Gently lower it into the shimmering green waters of the
Nagold that stared up at me from under the arc of the bridge.
Somewhere—I don't know its origin—in my blood, too, lay
An attraction to the secret of the depths, to fishes and
Fishing; standing on the riverbank I had already made
The first childish attempts at catching a fish with my hands,
Or, taking my mother's sewing things, I substituted
A length of yarn for the line and a bent pin for the fishhook.
Often the railing of the bridge was my chosen hunting
Ground, and the lame boy soon inadvertently became
A frequent neighbor and nearly a comrade, even if
At first the ironic gaze of his gray eyes, which smiling
Criticized my yarn and hook, myself and all I did,
Displeased me and hurt my feelings. For it was that lame boy,

Ja nicht bloß der Ältere, Erfahrne—in Dingen
 des Fischfangs
Und auch in andern wohl weit mir überlegen—, er war auch
Arm und elend gekleidet, Volksschüler, für den
 ich mit meiner
Blauen Lateinermütze ein Fremder und Spott war, ein Affe,
Herrensöhnchen und Feind, ich hatte das häufig erfahren,
Und obwohl meiner Eltern Leben bescheiden, mein Anzug
Häufig gestopft und das Schuhwerk mit manchen Flicken
 bedeckt war,
Kannte ich doch aus bittren Erlebnissen alle die Klüfte,
Alle die Gegnerschaften und bösen Schimpfworte,
 die zwischen
Jener Kaste und meiner beständig gefährliche Spannung
Aufrechterhielten, Bereitschaft zu Krieg, zu Angriff
 und Rache.
Dieser Lahme jedoch, trotz seiner ironischen Blicke,
Dachte an keinerlei Feindschaft, er war ja zum Kampf
 auch nicht tauglich.
Einmal kam ich vorüber, da zog er gerade an seiner
Straff gespannten Leine gewandt einen Fisch in die Höhe,
Blinzelte mir, der ich neugierig stehnblieb, listig
 und freundlich
Einen Augenblick zu aus schmalem Augenspalt, löste
Sanft das Fischlein vom Haken und hielt es mir
 lachend entgegen.
«Kennst du ihn?» fragte er mich, und da beschämt
 ich verneinte,
Höhnte er nicht, sondern hielt mir vors Auge den Fisch
 und erklärte

Not merely the elder, experienced one—in fishing
And other matters he far surpassed me—but the poor one,
Miserably dressed, a mere schoolboy, to whom I with my blue
Student cap was an alien, a laughingstock, a monkey,
A Little Lord Fauntleroy, a foe (I'd often felt this);
And even though my parents were of modest means,
      my clothes
Were often mended and my shoes had leather patches,
From bitter experience I knew all the rifts, all
The enmities and evil terms of abuse that preserved
The ever-present dangerous tension between his caste
And my own: readiness for war, assault and revenge.
But despite his ironic gaze, this lame boy had no thoughts
Of hostility; besides, he was hardly fit for fight.
Walking by, I once saw him tug at his taut line, skillfully
Pulling a fish into the air. While I stood there curious,
Out of his narrow eye-slit he winked at me a moment
Longer in a sly and friendly manner, and gently he took
The little fish off the hook and held it toward me laughing.
"Do you know this one?" he asked me; ashamed, I said no.
But he did not mock me; he held the fish before my eyes

Mir mit zeigenden Fingern und Worten Merkmal
 um Merkmal,
Trübgrüne Farbe des dunkelen Rückens und
 bläuliche Streifen,
Hellen fettschimmernden Bauch und die harten,
 stachlichten Flossen,
Barsch hieß der Fisch, so erfuhr ich, man nannt ihn
 auch Krätzer.
Barsch war trotz reichlicher Gräten ein leckerer Fisch, wenn
 auch längst nicht
Ebenbürtig dem Saibling und gar der edlen Forelle.
Da nun gebrochen das Eis der Fremdheit, so faßt ich
 ein Herz mir,
Lobte den Fisch ihm und pries bewundernd sein
 Können als Angler.
Freundlich darauf, mit dem Lächeln, das später an ihm
 mir so lieb ward,
Zeigte er mir seine Schnur, seinen Haken, und zog
 aus zerrißner
Jackentasche ein Ding hervor, ein blechernes Döschen,
Drin er den Köder verwahrte, die schlaff
 sich windenden Würmer.

So begann mein Verkehr mit dem Lahmen, und wurde
 in jenem
Sommer zu enger Gemeinschaft, denn unter Knaben
 wächst diese
Leicht aus Bewunderung, aber Bewunderung
 spendet ein Knabe

And with telling fingers and words explained mark after mark:
The muddy green color of its dusky back, the bluish stripes,
The bright belly pearly with fat, and the rigid, spiny fins;
Perch is the name of this fish, so I learned, true river perch.
Despite an abundance of bones, perch is a tasty fish,
Though of far lower birth than the char or the noble trout.
The ice of strangeness broken, I took heart, praised the fish
And admiring praised his ability as an angler.
Turned friendly, with that smile which later became so dear
To me, he showed me his string and his hook, and finally,
Out of his torn coat pocket he produced a small tin can,
In which the limp wriggling worms, the bait was secure.

The lame boy and I began to go around together;
Each summer our relationship grew closer, for among
Boys fellowship easily grows out of admiration,

Willig und ohne zu sparen, sobald ihm ein
    wirkliches Können,
Eine Vollendung in Kunst oder Fertigkeit irgend begegnet.
Mir begegnete sie, dem schüchtern beginnenden Fischer,
In der erstaunlichen Kunst des Älteren, Fische zu fangen.
Freilich die Anglerei, die wir beiden gemeinsam betrieben,
War urweltlich, barbarisch und primitiv wie von Wilden.
Wir entbehrten nicht nur des Gerätes, da war weder Rute
Noch auch Fischgarn, Glasschnur und Schwimmer, von
    künstlichen Fliegen
Hatten wir niemals vernommen, das einzige Instrument, das
Fertig im Laden wir kauften, waren die Haken,
Kleine stählerne Angeln, zwei Pfennig das Stück, und
    die größern
Kosteten drei—schon sie waren Fortschritt und Luxus,
    verglichen
Mit dem gefeilten Nagel, der rohgebogenen Nadel,
Die ich anfänglich verwendet. Es fehlte uns, sagt ich,
    nicht Garn nur,
Künstliche Rute und all dies nützliche Werkzeug,
Nein, es fehlte auch Lehre gänzlich und Vorbild. Mochten
    vor Zeiten
Andere in unsern Gewässern gefischt und vielleicht die
    Regeln des Fischens
Sportgerecht ausgeübt haben—wir konnten's nicht wissen.
Wir begannen, Knaben, als wäre die Welt erst
    gestern erschaffen.
Hier standen wir, auf der Brücke, am Ufer, am Rechen
    der Mühle,
Und dort unten im Feuchten, im Dunkeln hausten die Fische,

Which a boy spends freely as soon as true ability,
Perfection in an art, or dexterity comes his way.
A timid beginning fisherman, I admired
The elder boy's remarkable art of catching fish.
Of course, the fishing we did together was primeval,
Barbaric, primitive, like that of wild men.
Not only did we do without equipment—neither rods
Nor fishing line, tippets or floats were at hand; we knew
Nothing of artificial flies—the only instruments
That we bought ready-made in the store were the hooks, small
Steel hooks, two pennies apiece, and the larger cost three—
Even these were a luxury and a considerable
Advance over the filed nail, the crudely bent needle
I used at first. As I said, not only did we lack line,
Ready-made rods and all sorts of useful equipment,
We completely lacked a teacher and example. Others
Before us may well have fished in our waters, in fair sport
Abiding by the rules of fishing. We couldn't have known.
For us the world had been created only yesterday.
We stood on the bridge, or on the bank near the grate
        of the mill,
And below us in dampness, in darkness the fish dwelled;

Welchen nachzustellen ein eingeborener Jagdtrieb
Uns geheimnisvoll zwang. Denn der Mensch, solang ihn
   der Geist nicht
Wandelnd erzieht, ist gierig, ist Raubtier und Jäger; und
   spät erst,
Da ich schon größer wurde, begann das Fangen, das Quälen
Und das Töten der Fische mir wehzutun im Gewissen.

So denn nun, zwei Urmenschen mit primitivem Gelüsten,
Primitiven Mitteln betrieben wir Knaben den Fischfang,
Und da war es denn jener, der Lahme, der führte und lehrte,
Ohnehin älter als ich, und rätselhaft alt durch sein Leiden,
Das von den Menschen ihn trennte und ihren
   bevorzugten Freuden.
Nun aber war außerdem diesem lahmen Knaben vom Blut her
Sinn und Spürkraft verliehen für Flüsse und Bäche und alle
Ihre kühlen Bewohner, die silbernen Fische, die plumpen
Kroppen, die zähen Krebse. Er kannte sie alle und wußte
Ihre verborgenen Orte, ihr Leben und Brauchtum, und wußte
Mit allereinfachsten Mitteln zu locken sie und überlisten.
Manchmal, erinnr ich mich, stand ich mit meinem
   kindlichen Fischzeug
Irgendwo dort an der Nagold und hing meine Schnur
   ins Gewässer,
Er aber, wenn er dazu kam, schüttelte lächelnd den Kopf und
Sagte allwissend: «Du bist um gute zwei Stunden zu früh da,
Komm gegen Abend zurück, dann gibt es hier Barben
   und Barsche.»
Oder: «Es nützt dir nichts, an dieser Stelle mit Käse

An innate hunting instinct secretly made us lie
In wait for them. For man, as long as his restless spirit
Is not civilized, is greedy, a beast of prey, a hunter;
Only later, when I was somewhat older, did catching,
Tormenting and killing fish begin to trouble my conscience.

But back then, we were two primitives with primitive
Appetites, and with primitive means we boys went fishing.
The lame boy was my guide and my teacher, he was older
Than I, enigmatically old through his suffering that
Separated him from others and their normal pleasures.
But beyond this, the lame boy was endowed—it was in
His blood—with a power and sense for rivers and streams
And all their cool inhabitants, the silvery fish,
The clumsy miller's-thumbs, the tenacious crabs. He knew
Them all, knew where they hid, their life and habits,
      and knew
How to lure and outwit them with the simplest of means.
I remember how I'd stand with my childish fishing tackle
Somewhere on the Nagold, hanging my string in the waters;
When he found me there, he'd smile, shake his head and say,
All-knowing, "You're here a good two hours early;
Come back toward evening, then there'll be barbel and perch."
Or, "It'll do you no good to bait your hook with cheese or

Oder mit Brot zu ködern, nimm Fliegen!» Und siehe,
    sein Rat war
Jedesmal gut. Und er konnte ein andres Mal sagen:
    «Da stehst du,
Immer die Schnur in der Hand und immerzu fischst du
    und fischest!
Aber man muß nicht bloß fischen, man muß auch
    schlendern und schauen,
Muß das Aug und die Nase spazieren führen. Dort drunten
Nah bei der Insel, ich wette, stehn jetzt im
    Seegras verborgen
Rotaugen mehr als genug, die Mäuler gegen die Strömung.
Fangen kannst du sie nicht, es ist nicht die Stunde,
    doch schauen
Wollen wir sie.» Und ich haspelte denn meine
    Schnüre zusammen,
Ging mit ihm, und wir schlichen am Ufer abwärts,
    und plötzlich
Blieb er stehn wie gebannt, ins Wasser starrend, dann blitzt' er
Mich aus halbgeschlossenem Auge so an und hob
    sachte den Finger,
Meine Blicke zu lenken, und siehe, auch mir ward
    das Auge geöffnet:
Dunkel im bräunlich-goldenen, leise wogenden Seegras
Standen die schmalen Rücken der Fische. Die Strömung
    war kräftig,
Regungslos aber verharrten die Tiere, der Strömung entgegen
Fast unmerklich die Flossen rührend, dem Seegras
    verschwistert,
Und nur selten etwa geschah es einmal, daß ein Fisch sich

With bread here; use flies!" And you see, his advice was good
Every time. Some other time he might say, "There you stand,
Your string always in your hand, always fishing and fishing!
But you can't just fish, you must loiter and be on the lookout;
You have to take your eyes and your nose out for a walk.
Under there, near the island, I'll bet there are plenty of
Roach hidden in the eelgrass, their mouths against the current.
But you can't catch them, it's not the right time; still
        we ought to take
A look at them." Then I rolled up my string and
        went with him;
We sneaked down the bank, and suddenly he stood
        there staring
Into the water, as if rooted to the spot; through half-closed
Eyes he gave me a sharp look, cautiously raised a finger
To direct my gaze; and see, even my eyes were opened:
Dark in the brownish-golden, gently swaying eelgrass
Were the narrow backs of the fish. The current was strong,
But the fish remained motionless, moving their fins almost
Imperceptibly against it, as if bound to the eelgrass.
Seldom—it may have happened once—a fish would begin

Weich im Flusse zu drehen anhob und daß statt des schmalen
    und dunkeln
Rückens die breite silberne Flanke schwach
    leuchtete und auch
Uns das Auge, das kupferfarbne, anblickte und schleunig
Wieder verschwand. O da sah oft in kurzen Sekunden
    das wilde
Rätsel der Kreatur uns an, und erlosch, und wir standen
Tief aufgeregt, aber starr und schweigend, bis
    Alltag und Straße
Wieder den alten Singsang sangen und wir uns ernüchtert,
Ja verlegen mit künstlichem Lachen und Räuspern
    zurück zum
Rätsellosen und Oftgesehenen wandten. Ich lernte
Vieles und Schönes damals vom Kameraden, dem Lahmen.

War mir in vielem, in allem voraus der andre, so war er's
In der Geduld doch besonders. Die edle Tugend, mir war sie
Nicht gegeben, ich habe um sie zeitlebens gemüht mich
Und in Jahrzehnten nur und nur stümperhaft so viel erworben,
Als es zur Not bedarf. Und als Knabe war ich besonders
Ungeduldig im Kleinen, Alltäglichen, ging mit den Sachen,
Ging mit dem An- und Ausziehn, dem Schnüren der Schuhe,
    dem Werkzeug
Wenig liebevoll um. Statt dessen hatte mein Freund nun
Ein Paar hagere Hände mit dünnen, fast spinnigen Fingern,
Die ich oft fleißig und emsig, doch niemals hastend gesehen,
Freundlich faßten sie zu und liebevoll. Knoten zu schürzen
Oder zu lösen fiel ihnen leicht, und wenn es passierte,

To turn gently in the river; instead of its dark
Narrow back its broad silver flanks shone feebly and its
Copper-colored eye looked at us and quickly vanished again.
O, how often, in a few brief seconds, the wild riddle
Of the creature lit on us and burned out, and we stood
Deeply moved, but stiff and silent, until the weekday and
The street sang their old singsong, and we came to our senses;
Embarrassed, with false laughter, clearing our throats, we
      turned back
To the Unenigmatic and the Often-seen; I learned so much,
So much beauty in those days from my comrade, the lame boy.

As he surpassed me in many things, in all, he did so
Especially in patience. The noble virtue was not
Given to me; all my life I have taken great pains to
Acquire it, in decades only bunglingly won so much
As necessity required. And as a boy I was
Particularly impatient with little, everyday things;
I was not very careful dressing and undressing,
Lacing my shoes, working with tools. In contrast, my friend
Had a pair of bony hands with thin, nearly spidery
Fingers that I'd often seen diligent and active at work,
Never hasty, they did everything with loving care.
Tying or untying knots was easy for them, and once

Daß uns einmal das Fischgarn sich durch ein
    Unglück verwirrte,
Griffen die allzudünnen, doch sicheren Finger behutsam
In den schrecklichen Knäuel, vor dem ich beinah
    schon verzweifelt,
Rückten, legten und schoben und lockerten
    sachte die Knoten,
Welches zumal bei frisch aus dem Wasser
    gezogenen Schnüren
Gar nicht so leicht ist, und bald war alles
    reinlich geschlichtet.
Dieser Meister nun war's der Geduld und der Knoten,
    der freundlich,
Unermüdlich mich unterwies. Er lehrte mich vierfach
Schwarzes Nähgarn in halber Armeslänge ans Ende
Meiner Angelschnur knüpfen und an das Garn
    dann die Angel,
Lehrte gerissene Schnüre mich flicken, und wirklich,
    ich lernt es,
Ich, den bislang die Magd wie die Mutter vergeblich
    bemüht war,
Etwas Ordnung zu lehren in Schrank und Wäsche.
    Ich lernt es,
Weil das Endziel der Mühe, der Fischfang, mir wichtig
    und lieb war,
Aber nicht minder auch weil der Lehrer meine Bewundrung,
Ja, und auch meine Liebe besaß. Aber dennoch war es
    nicht Freundschaft,
Was uns zwei Knaben sommerlang innig verband. Wir waren
    nicht Freunde.

When the fishing line accidentally got entangled,
The all too thin but sure fingers carefully took hold of
The terrible clew, before which I'd almost given up hope,
Tugged at it, put it down, slid and loosened the knot
    by degrees—
Which is not very easy to do with strings just drawn out
Of the water—and soon everything was neatly unraveled.
This master of patience and knots amiably and
Tirelessly instructed me. He taught me to attach
Half an arm's length of quadrupled black thread to the end
Of my fishing line, and onto the thread's end the fishhook;
He taught me how to mend torn lines, and I actually learned,
I, who until then neither the maid nor my mother could
Teach to straighten up my wardrobe or dresser, I learned
Because the final aim of the effort, catching fish, was
Important and dear to me. But not less because the teacher
Possessed my admiration and my love. And yet, it was
Not friendship that inwardly bound us boys
    the whole summer.

Nicht ein einzig Mal sah ich ihn bei mir im Haus
    meines Vaters,
Spielte unsere Spiele mit ihm oder zeigt ihm den Garten,
Zeigt ihm den Saal und die Bibliothek. Und ebenso bin ich
Niemals bei ihm zu Besuch oder Gast gewesen, ich wußte
Zwar den Hof, wo er wohnte, doch kannt ich das Haus und
    die Tür nicht.
Seine Welt war nicht meine, es ward nicht von
    Vater und Mutter,
Nicht von Schule und Spielkameraden gesprochen,
    ja selbst nicht
Seines Gebrechens geschah Erwähnung; nur einmal
Ließ er mich sehn die «Maschine», den Bau aus
    Eisen und Leder,
Der ihm das Bein einschnürte, mir den Mechanismus
    erklärend.
Auch von andren Dingen, die mir oder ihm wohl zuzeiten
Herz und Seele mochten bewegen, sprachen wir selten,
Und wenn es einmal geschah, so war ich staunender Hörer,
Denn er redete ganz wie Erwachsene, sicher und alle
Diskussionen im Keime erstickend. So sprach er mir einmal
Kühl und ein wenig zynisch vom Tode. Da «strecke» man sich
    und sei fertig,
Und es folge nichts nach, denn das, was die
    Pfaffen erzählten,
Nehme ein Mann und Wissender ernst nicht, es sei
    nur Geschwatze.
Mir blieb die Antwort aus, ich war ja kein Mann, war
    ein Kind noch,

We were not friends. Not once did I receive him in
    my father's
House; not once did we play our games with him, or show him
The garden, the reception hall, or the library. Nor
Had I ever visited his home. I knew only
The courtyard he lived off, but not which doorway was his.
His world was not mine; we didn't talk about our parents,
Or discuss our schoolmates and playmates, and no mention
Was made of his handicap. Only once did he let me
See the "machine"—explaining its mechanism to me—
The construct of iron and leather that hemmed in his leg.
We seldom spoke of other things, even those which at times
Might well have moved our hearts and our souls. And when
    we once did,
I was an astonished listener, for he talked just like
An adult, self-assured, nipping all discussion in the bud.
Cool and somewhat cynical, he spoke to me about death.
You "lie down" and are done for, and nothing comes
    afterwards,
For what the priests have described, a man, a knowing man
Can not take seriously; it's just meaningless chatter.
I made no answer, I was not a man, was still a child

Das den Eltern vertraut und dem lieben Gott.
    Sein Bekenntnis
Dünkte mir männlich und kam aus Gebieten der Seele,
    in die ich
Kaum einen Schritt noch getan. Wir waren also
    nicht Freunde,
Waren unendlich weit voneinander. Und dennoch
    verband uns
Ein Geheimnis und Zauber zwei Sommer lang fest,
    Kameraden
Sind wir gewesen und einig in einem Triebe und Streben,
Einem einzigen nur, doch es band uns lange und innig.

Wunderlich war dieses Knaben Erwachsensein: Das
    Gesicht schien
Alt, ja zuweilen fast greise, und war doch unfertig
    und heimlich
Voll noch von Kindheit, die Züge klein und die Haut zwar
Bleich und etwas gefaltet, doch jugendlich zart. Jenes Fremde,
Greise und Gnomische lag in den Augen allein und
    dem Munde,
In der reifen Stille des Blicks und der bitteren
    Herbe des Mundes.
Hager und spitz war das Kinn und scharf
    die Kiefer gewinkelt,
Alles Knochenwerk schien vom Fleisch nur lose bekleidet,
In der Stirn von Braue zu Brau' eine Falte gezogen
Und zwei tiefre zu beiden Seiten vom Winkel des Mundes
Schräg nach unten: ein Antlitz, bedeutend gezeichnet

Who trusted in my parents and in the good Lord. His
Confession seemed manly, came from regions of the soul
In which I had scarcely set foot. Thus, we were not friends,
Were infinitely far from one another. And yet
Mystery and magic bound us fast for two summers, we
Became comrades united in one drive, one endeavor,
Only one; still it bound us long and intimately.

The boy's adulthood was strange: his face seemed old, at times
Almost hoary, and yet immature, mysteriously
Full of childhood; his features were small, his skin
          pale, somewhat
Wrinkled, yet youthfully soft. A strange, hoary, gnomic
Quality lay in his eyes and his mouth: in the ripe
Stillness of his gaze and the bitter severity
Of his mouth. His chin was lean and pointed, his jaw sharp,
Angular; his skeleton seemed only loosely clad with flesh;
A deep line marked his forehead from eyebrow to eyebrow,
And two deeper lines slanted down from the corners of
His mouth: a countenance strikingly marked as much by

So von Geist wie von Leide, darunter dürftig die schiefe,
Etwas verwachsne Gestalt mit zu hohen Schultern, getragen
Von dem verkümmerten Beinwerk mit Hilfe von Stock
    und «Maschine».
So erscheint er mir manchmal, mein Fischkamerad,
    den ich später
Ganz unmerklich verlor, noch ehe der Tod ihn, noch Knabe,
Wegnahm. Er zeigt sich am liebsten an schwülen Tagen
    im Sommer,
Wenn das Ufer stark riecht und aus Wasser und
    Seegras zuweilen
Blasen steigen und platzen, auch manchmal über den Spiegel
Wie in suchender Qual ein kleinerer Fisch sich ans
    Licht schnellt
Oder ein größerer schwer mit aufblinkendem Schwanze
    emporschnalzt.
Trage ich Schuld, daß wir damals, zwei Fremde, uns einzig
Unterm kühlen Zeichen der Fische begegneten, daß
    keine Freundschaft
Uns geglückt ist? Hätt ich, dein dankbarer Lehrling,
    trotz allem
Dich herüberlocken und zwingen sollen in meine
Welt, oder dich in die deine hinüber verfolgen,
In die modrigen Höfe, die finstern ärmlichen Häuser,
Wo auch du, Einsamer, doch eine Heimat hattest?
    Du hast mich
Niemals darum gebeten. Warst du schon damals so wissend,
Daß du den Abgrund kanntest, dem unsre
    Verbindung entblühte,
Der sie wieder verschlang? Ich denke mir gerne, du seiest

Spirit as by suffering; below it the haggard, bent,
Somewhat deformed figure with overhigh shoulders, borne
By the stunted leg with the aid of a crutch and "machine."
That's how he looked to me sometimes, my fishing
   companion, whom
I later lost without a trace, even before death took him,
Still a boy. He liked best to come out on sultry summer days
When the bank had a strong smell, and bubbles rose
   through the water
And eelgrass and burst; or sometimes above the surface
   a small
Fish, as if in searching torment, darted into the light, or
A larger one with exertion snapped up its sparkling tail.
Am I to blame that for us alone, two strangers back then,
Who met under the cool sign of The Fish, no friendship was
Possible? Should I, your appreciative student, in spite
Of all, have enticed you and forced you into my world,
Or have followed you over into yours, into the
Musty courtyards, the miserable gloomy houses,
Where you, too, solitary one, still had a home? You
Never invited me. Were you already so knowing
That you acknowledged the gulf in which our bond arose
And which swallowed it again? I like to think that you

Heimlich ein Fisch- und Zwergen- und
    Wasserkönig gewesen,
Unter die Menschen verirrt, und hoffe, daß du zurückfandst
In die kühlen Schauer und Kostbarkeiten der Tiefe,
Heim in die Welt aus Silber und Feuchte und
    goldenem Dunkel,
Wo von der Strömung gekämmt das lange
    Flußgras dahinwallt.

1937

Secretly were a king of fishes and dwarves and waters,
Lost among people, and I hope you have found your way back
To the cool deep-water currents and treasures, at home
In the world of silver and moisture and golden darkness,
Where, combed by the current, the tall river grass sways.

1937

Skizzenblatt

❦

Kalt knistert Herbstwind im dürren Rohr,
Das im Abend ergraut ist;
Krähen flattern vom Weidenbaume landeinwärts.

Einsam steht und rastet am Strande ein alter Mann,
Spürt den Wind im Haar, die Nacht und nahenden Schnee,
Blickt vom Schattenufer ins Lichte hinüber,
Wo zwischen Wolke und See ein Streifen
Fernsten Strandes noch warm im Lichte leuchtet:
Goldenes Jenseits, selig wie Traum und Dichtung.

Fest im Auge hält er das leuchtende Bild,
Denkt der Heimat, denkt seiner guten Jahre,
Sieht das Gold erbleichen, sieht es erlöschen,
Wendet sich ab und wandert
Langsam vom Weidenbaume landeinwärts.

Dezember 1946

Sketch

Fall wind crackles cold in the sere reeds
That are gray in the evening;
From the willow tree crows float inland.

Standing alone, resting on the shore, an old man
Feels the wind in his hair, the night, the snow that will fall,
From the shadowy shore looks over into the light,
Where, between cloud bank and lake, a strip
Of the far shore still gleams warm in the light:
Golden beyond, blessed as dream, as creation.

He holds the luminous image fixed in his sight,
Thinks of his homeland, thinks of his good full years,
Sees the gold pale, sees it fade out,
Turns away, and slowly
From the willow tree wanders inland.

December 1946

Knarren eines geknickten Astes

❧❧

Splittrig geknickter Ast,
Hangend schon Jahr um Jahr
Trocken knarrt er im Wind sein Lied,
Ohne Laub, ohne Rinde,
Kahl, fahl, zu langen Lebens,
Zu langen Sterbens müd.
Hart klingt und zäh sein Gesang,
Klingt trotzig, klingt heimlich bang
Noch einen Sommer, noch einen Winter lang.

August 1962

Creaking of a Broken Bough

Brittle broken bough,
Hanging year after year
Dryly its song groans in the wind,
Leafless, stripped of bark,
Bare, blanched, tired of living
Too long, of dying too long, tired.
Its song sounds harsh and stubborn,
Sounds defiant, secretly alarmed
One more summer, one more winter long.

August 1962